INFLUENCER MARKETING:

The ultimate guide on how to make use of influencer marketing for your brand

BY

KAREN COLEMAN

TABLE OF CONTENTS

CHAPTER ONE

CHAPTER TWO

CHAPTER THREE

CHAPTER ONE

INFLUENCER MARKETING IS TAKING OVER ONLINE ADVERTISING

Marketing is changing. Public relations and advertising don't seem to be as effective as they once were. People no longer only base their purchasing choices on print or web marketing. This is because the internet's easy access to information has given this generation the power to control their purchasing. More than ever, they prefer to do their homework, watch tutorial videos, read reviews, and hear from other people before making a purchase. How do entrepreneurs and marketers respond to these developments in consumer spending? Influencer marketing is the secret.

Influencer marketing: What is it?
Influencer marketing is a style of advertising where marketers communicate with their audience through leaders in a related niche or group rather than directly with them. Consumers are more reluctant than ever to believe in direct brand messaging with a sales-driven tone, which is why influencers are crucial in today's market. Instead, they rely on the respected online peers they follow.

Influencers are thought leaders who have already won the audience a business is attempting to reach trust. They have achieved this by acting as intermediaries and disseminating their information and ideas purely out of a desire to assist others. Influencers use their creative talents to publish amusing, educational, and value-driven material on social media platforms. Influencers win the loyalty of devoted followers after a period of persistent content development and promotion. In conclusion, a person who has influence is one who has often amassed over 10,000 followers.

Brands interact to market their goods, services, or message.

shares details on the goods, companies, and causes they support.

acts as a specialist in their field.

UNDERSTANDING THE KINDS OF INFLUENCERS

Entrepreneurs and business owners when they locate the proper influencers to work with, brands make more than five times what they invest in doing so.

Finding the right kind of influencers to help the company get actual results is the first difficulty. especially with the option of five different influencer types.

Here are five types of influencers:

Mega-influencers with a following of more than a million (think celebrities).

Macro-influencers who have between 500K and 1M followers.

Intermediate Influencers in the middle, between 50K and 500K followers micro-influencers with between 10K and 50K fans

1K to 10K follower nano-influencers.

So how do you choose which influencers are most suitable for your brand? You spend some time getting to know each one, thinking about how they are, and comparing the advantages to your business objectives. Here is a list of the top 5 influencer categories from which you may pick the one that best suits your brand:

- Mega-Influencers
- Macro-Influencers
- Intermediate Influencers
- Micro-Influencers
- Nano-Influencers

Mega-Influencers

Mega-influencers, who have more than a million followers, are well known on social media because of their celebrity status. They produce a ton of engagement on the social media channels where their audience is engaged. This is what makes them desirable to organizations looking to utilize influencer marketing, as well as what drives up their cost.

Point to note: The rate of engagement declines as an influencer's overall number of followers increases, although mega-influencers have a tremendous reach. The engagement rate for Instagram influencers with more than 10 million followers is only 1.6%.

Macro-Influencers

Macro-influencers are those who have an audience of 500,000 to 1 million or more and can include thought leaders, athletes, celebrities, and TV personalities. Brands may anticipate a high price tag from them because they can use their reputation to get followers on social media, however, it won't be as expensive as with mega-influencers. With this kind of influencer, brands can still reach a wide audience, but they might not get the engagement they are looking for. This is because of the previously mentioned follower-to-engagement ratio.

Points to note: Compared to content produced by micro- or nano-influencers, macro-influencer content often has a more polished appearance. This might be a better fit for some brands' audiences and objectives.

Intermediate Influencers

Despite not having celebrity status, mid-tier influencers are nevertheless a significant group of content producers whose followers have faith in them. In comparison to macro- or mega-influencers, these influencers provide marketers with a broad reach and a little bit higher engagement with audiences between 50K and 500K. Each post has authentic, up-to-date content that is polished but not dated.

Points to note: Mid-tier influencers presumably spent years moving up the ranks from nano-influencer to intermediate influencers rather than using popularity to ascend quickly. They have a lot of experience producing content and have a stronger connection to their audience.

Micro-Influencers

Micro-influencers are often seen by marketers as being significantly more effective in terms of engagement and trust, despite having a much smaller audience than mega-influencers. That's because micro-influencers are more specialized and have a close relationship with their fans and followers. A product recommended by a micro-influencer is more likely to be purchased by 82 percent of consumers.

Considerations: Compared to content from macro- or mega-influencers, micro-influencer content is less polished but may come across as more genuine. Depending on the company's objectives, this could affect the level of success it has with influencer marketing

Nano-Influencers

Nano-influencers, who have the fewest followers, give marketers a tiny and likely smaller reach. What businesses do lose in reach, however, they make up for in interaction rates. With an engagement rate of 8.8%, nano-influencers lead all other influencer types. Because the content is so authentic and tailored to the audience, marketers dealing with this kind of influencer can anticipate a unique experience.

Considerations: Because nano-influencers are far more cost-effective than their larger counterparts, firms with limited funding may wish to begin their influencer marketing campaigns with them. Some nano-influencers even work for free to gain brand relationships and grow their fan base.

CHAPTER TWO

BEFORE PAYING YOUR SOCIAL MEDIA INFLUENCER

Although social media and content marketing are useful tools for connecting with customers, most firms only have a small audience. Once a company has established a profile, it will begin to communicate with many of the same people frequently. A company needs to regularly reach out to new customers if it wants to significantly increase its bottom line. This necessitates turning to influencers for publicity for many brands. Influencers can reach a big audience at once and are typically described as online personalities with a sizable or loyal following. However, brands err by concentrating only on a person's number of followers. Here are seven qualities an influencer should have that can assist your company find the appropriate one.

1. What are your brand objectives and what kind of influencers that fit into it.

As a brand, you understand the end goal of your brand and the value that your brand and products communicate. You do not want to be associated with influencers who's activities differ from your brand objectives. Search for influencers who's activities and contents works well with your objectives as a brand.

2. Compatible followers.

In terms of conversions, simple numbers are not very meaningful. In general, it is true that a person's online behaviors may result in more engagement for the many companies they discuss the more followers they have. However, even if an influencer has hundreds of thousands of followers, marketing to them is usually a waste of time if their audience isn't interested in your brand. Even if they have less followers than other influencers, find influencers whose audience fits your own target demographics.

3. Celebrity status.

"Celebrity" takes many different shapes in the online world. Even more so if that celebrity has a sizable following in another medium, a celebrity who engages on social media has a considerably wider reach than someone who doesn't. Of course there are stars in movies and on television, but reality show stars are also well-known and frequently interact with their followers online, which increases engagement. Musicians that interact with their enormous fan bases can be very successful ambassadors for occasions like music festivals. Bloggers and popular YouTubers can also have a sizable online following that may be useful to brands. In many cases, contacting an Internet celebrity is more successful for a company than contacting an actor, singer, or reality show star.

4. The posts' content.

Examine an influencer's postings carefully before getting in touch to see if the frequently updated content is appropriate for your brand. It's conceivable that some social media influencers present an online persona that conflicts with your own. To ensure there won't be any unpleasant surprises when your partnership launches, look through an influencer's earlier posts and read them carefully.

5. A social networking site.

Whether it's the image-based content on Pinterest or the brief videos on Vine, every brand has a preferred social media channel. Influencers on Instagram operate very differently from "power users" on Twitter. Instagram caters to a younger audience and is almost entirely visual in nature, whereas Twitter leans older and is perhaps best known for being a platform for sharing news stories, frequently about business, sports, or entertainment. Determine the ideal platform for your brand and seek out an influencer who is an expert there.

6. Audience engagement.

Social networking facilitates two-way communication when done properly. A good brand influencer engages with other users online in addition to posting great content. Because of their consistent interaction, followers are more inclined to pay attention to advice.

7. Previous brand behavior.

Consider past brand initiatives in particular as you examine an influencer's previous content. What tactics did the influencer use to market additional goods? Your study will not only help you eliminate social media users who won't give your brand the boost it needs, but it will also serve as an excellent starting point for your conversation with the influencer. "I admire what you did for (Brand X) and would love something similar for my product launch," you'll be able to say.

8. Results.

After you've chosen your influencer and started working, you must track your progress. Find the analytics tool that best suits your influencer-based marketing initiatives by doing research on a range of them, including GoogleAnalytics, Buzzstarter, and 33Across. You'll be able to precisely characterize your accomplishments and failures as you go along and base future influencer searches on them.

SETTING INFLUENCER MARKETING GOALS

As a brand, you should use influencer marketing now that you understand what it is and why it is important. The next step is to develop campaign goals before investing your hard-earned money.

The acquisition of profitable customers is probably the ultimate marketing objective of any brand. But there are numerous ways to accomplish that.

What position does influencer marketing occupy? Influencers may boost a brand's overall visibility, social media profile, website and product page traffic, initial orders, repeat purchase rates, higher-margin purchases, average order size, and other factors.

It may seem like a daunting process. Think about the SMART and BSQ goal-setting frameworks as a starting point.

BSQ

- **B** – Think of a *big* goal.
- **S** – *Small* actions make up the big goal.
- **Q** – Move *quickly*, or it won't matter.

According to David Van Rooney, a writer, scholar, and vice president at Walmart, BSQ establishes a straightforward yet effective long-term focus, divided into more manageable tasks.

An e-commerce marketer, for instance, would wish to boost sales to a certain product page. Increasing XYZ product sales by 300 percent can be written in the B section of the framework.

Four influencer actions could be included in the S portion: (i) two business-related mega influencer celebrities to promote the product on their Instagram profiles for immediate visibility and potential traffic. (ii) ten credible macro influencers to analyze the celebrity endorsements on YouTube and discuss the merits of the product while encouraging comments. (iii). 10 more intermediate influencers buy the product and post their opinions on each channel of the preceding pyramid of influence.

(iv) 10 additional micro influencers to share the YouTube videos on their Facebook and Twitter accounts with a brief affirmation of why they agree.

It is possible to move fast on the first item of the sequence by breaking the goal down into actions. BSQ is a time saver where a quick and good goal is better than no goal at all.

SMART

Although quick and logical, BSQ allows for some ambiguity. SMART, developed by training platform Smart Insights, is a more advanced framework for creating goals.

- S – Make your goal *specific*.
- M – Your goal must be *measurable*.

- A – Your goal needs to be *attainable* (or *actionable*).
- R – *Relevancy* is key.
- T – Create a fixed *timetable*.

An issue with BSQ is addressed by the relevance-focused approach of SMART. A marketer could start an influencer campaign with BSQ by taking a simple, rapidly accomplishable action.

However, it could not be important to the outcome.

For instance, if a firm isn't posting product information on YouTube, paying 50 YouTube influencers to ask their followers to like and subscribe to the brand's YouTube page won't help increase sales.

Similar to the BSQ trap, where it is easy to start a little activity that isn't likely to happen, the attainability factor on SMART addresses this issue.

The Mega influencers, for instance, may not have been a hire that the company could ever afford.

Creating Campaigns

Brands may approach all marketing efforts, influencer, and non-influencer, more effectively if they have a clear end objective and a breakdown of their tasks.

Use influencers to get more for your money by:

- Generosity is a good way to get more for your money when using influencers. A typical mistake is to underestimate influencers. It can occasionally be successful, but brands frequently overlook the need for brand ambassadors. Influencers who receive appropriate compensation are much more likely to leave positive ratings. View influencers as partners, not used car salespeople.

- Repurposing:
The cost of marketing can add up. Try to repurpose content you've acquired from an influencer across other platforms. Blog about a YouTube review that you have transcribed. The blog article should be edited into Instagram stories, and those stories should then be made into still photos for Pinterest.

- Amplifying: You may significantly increase the impact of an excellent review across other marketing channels and audiences by linking and combining the influencers' efforts.

Track your campaign

So, you have made it this far and your campaign is online. Congratulations! Now you will want to keep a careful watch on your campaign while it is running.

After your thorough preparation, it is crucial not to drop the ball at this level. Conversations on social media may evolve rapidly, so you will need to keep a careful watch on the campaign development and how people are responding to the material. Make careful to monitor critical metrics like:

Reaches, engagements and Sales.

Don't forget to monitor the content production of your influencers as well. Have they uploaded the agreed upon content pieces?.

Ensure you track what influencers are saying about your business, how their audiences are reacting – and whether rivals have responded to your campaign.

Report, analyze & evaluate

The last stage of the procedure is to measure the outcomes and gather the learnings. Did you meet your campaign goals? Create reports of the partnerships with all essential performance data and attempt to discover any similarities so you will know next time what sort of content and which influencers to concentrate on.

CHAPTER THREE

MAXIMIZE YOUR REVIEWS FOR MORE EXPOSURE

After making use of influencer marketing strategies, make the most use of the reviews you got using influencers, as it gives your brand more exposure. Whether you're ready for it or not, both your current customers and potential consumers enjoy leaving and reading online reviews.

Online reviews are now pervasive. They are now present on more websites than only review sites. They can be found and seen on social media sites like Facebook as well as Google search. Online reviews might seem intimidating and challenging to manage if you're new to the online business world. You might be tempted to ignore them because they are "just there" or "nice to have."

The bad news is that customers heavily rely on them to guide their purchasing decisions. Unbelievably, reviews are said to be viewed before a purchase by 90% of American shoppers. The good news is that businesses have many chances to boost exposure and sway potential customers thanks to the proliferation of online reviews. Monitoring online reviews is essential for both managing your online reputation and expanding your business.

Here are some ways on how to use internet reviews to your advantage and use them to enhance your marketing, sales, and customer experience if you don't want to be too late to the party.

1. To boost the visibility of your brand, use reviews

Reviews found online are the new word-of-mouth. Good reviews boost your visibility and make it easier for clients to find you, so the more the better. Here are some specific ways reviews can increase the visibility of your brand:

Reviews make you more noticeable in search

Reviews of your company don't merely speak to the quality of your goods and services. They also affect how well you rank in searches. A customer's assessment of a company and its products results in original, recent content. Your listing moves in the results because fresh content is adored by search engines. Having excellent reviews also makes you more visible in "best...in..." searches:

Google even enables AdWords users to integrate reviews into their ads. Once more, these blurbs make your listing stand out to clients who are comparing goods or services:

On some websites like Booking.com, you can rate results in addition to using search engines by how many reviews they have received. Similarly, you can find tools by their ranking on review websites for business tools:

Reviews can significantly enhance your visibility across platforms and make you more discoverable to buyers.

Take charge of your reviews gotten from influencers pages and social media accounts by, for example, ensuring that reviews are enabled on your Facebook page and other platforms and motivating as many clients to post you evaluations as you can.

When choosing keywords for your goods, consult client reviews.

By focusing on your keyword targeting and examining how customers describe your items in their reviews, you can take a more proactive approach to expanding the reach of your brand. This helps you get a better idea of how buyers view and look for your products. You might believe yourself to be a social media tool, for instance, but your users might see or use you more as an influencer marketing tool. You can have a better understanding of how to enhance your product positioning, long-tail keyword targeting, tags, or content production and help your business rank higher in search, whether it be on Google, TripAdvisor, or Amazon, by keeping track of the popular keywords used by customers in reviews.

Utilize favorable comments in your PR and influencer outreach.
Influencers want to be linked with well-known brands because they have reputations to maintain. Influencers know how much people love your brand and why they would profit from working with you. Everyone wants to be friends with those who are well-liked and popular. So, in your

subsequent pitch email, mention those five-star reviews.
Being modest or shy at this time is inappropriate.

2. Increase sales by using online reviews

Nine out of ten customers read reviews before making a purchase, as you are already aware. But did you realize that consumers will spend more if they read positive reviews? Supply and demand really is all there is to it. The higher your costs can be, the more people will like you. Therefore, if you aren't using them to increase sales, you're essentially throwing money away. Utilize favorable evaluations as social proof.

Use your well-earned 5-star reviews if you have them! Show everyone! Include them in the emails you use to prospect for sales. Affix them to your webpage. Tell others where to find them and that they are there.

Salvage bad reviews

Strangely, bad reviews are also helpful. Customers are wary of brands that only have positive ratings, and 67 percent of customers have more faith in a brand when they read both positive and negative evaluations.
Some people think that consumers who actively seek out negative evaluations are more involved in their pre-purchase research and are significantly more likely to make a purchase.

Regardless of whether negative customer feedback boosts conversion rates, you can train your sales staff to treat it as an objection and develop better objection management strategies for future clients. Your sales representatives will have a better chance of closing more deals if they are more knowledgeable about potential deal-breakers.

3. Improve your product with customer feedback

The most effective place to gather product feedback is through customer reviews. What your target market likes, dislikes, and thinks you should change about your product is exactly what they are telling you.

The following are some particular ways you can use customer reviews to enhance your product:

Identify and fix bugs. Customers frequently find product issues before you do. Additionally, they might like to inform you and potential clients through online reviews. Spot these complaints early on and address them as soon as possible.

Investigate patterns. Assess the negative reviews and find the common denominators. What is it that they all agree is so awful? Examine your customer feedback to identify a recurring theme, then change your product accordingly.

Give them more of what they desire. What qualities do your customers adore? How do they employ your goods? This information is beneficial for products that are still under development. Alternatively, if your product team wants to remove or add features. observe the opposition. Online reviews of your competitors' products can provide you with just as much, if not more, information about how to improve your own. What aspects of them do customers love and dislike? What can you take away from their successes and failures?

4. Boost client satisfaction by reading online reviews

Reviews have unavoidably evolved into another route for customer care as more customers vent their frustrations and share their experiences online. If you want to boost customer happiness and loyalty, you must remain on top of online reviews and

reach out in time to demonstrate to them
you care.

Address all grievances
Although it might seem obvious, a
surprising number of f brands choose to
disregard online complaints.
Naturally, giving your clients the impression
that they are speaking to a brick wall won't
help you retain them. I personally feel so
irritated when businesses ignore my concern
that I submit more reviews on other
platforms in an effort to gain their attention.
The majority of clients are aware that issues
cannot always be resolved right away, but
they still require reassurance that you have
heard them and are making an effort to find
a solution.

Utilize the chance to establish a rapport with clients.

Positive reviews should also be addressed. Customers are encouraged to continue interacting with your brand and may even end up supporting it. It can be as easy as giving a satisfied consumer significant attention:

Utilize user-generated FAQs like reviews

The majority of people enjoy sharing their experiences with others, which can assist you in developing a user-generated FAQ that explains how to use your product, what to watch out for, how to select various items depending on your needs, etc.

Customers who are on the fence or who have related inquiries may find your client testimonials to be useful information. A wonderful system is in place at Amazon to promote user-generated FAQs: You can add a similar review/FAQ section to your website or encourage users of review sites and social media platforms to use their built-in review features.

Utilize the influence of internet reviews

As you can see, there are countless ways internet reviews can assist you increase sales, marketing, product development, and customer satisfaction.

Allowing all of these opportunities to pass you by and end up in the hands of your rivals is just such a terrible waste.

www.ingramcontent.com/pod-product-compliance
Lightning Source LLC
Chambersburg PA
CBHW051937150726
47999CB00006B/2253